CLEOPATRA

"SERPENT OF THE NILE"

By Mary Fisk Pack | Illustrated by Peter Malone

goosebottombooks

© 2011 Goosebottom Books LLC

Series editor **Shirin Yim Bridges**
Editor **Amy Novesky**
Copy editor **Jennifer Fry**
Editorial assistant **Ann Edwards**
Book design **Jay Mladjenovic**

Typeset in Trajan, Ringbearer, Volkswagen, and Gill Sans
Illustrations rendered in gouache

Manufactured in Singapore

Library of Congress Control Number: 2011924335

ISBN: 978-0-9834256-0-1

First Edition   10 9 8 7 6 5 4 3 2 1

Goosebottom Books LLC
710 Portofino Lane, Foster City, CA 94404

www.goosebottombooks.com

The Thinking Girl's Treasury of Dastardly Dames

CLEOPATRA
"SERPENT OF THE NILE"

AGRIPPINA
"ATROCIOUS AND FEROCIOUS"

MARY TUDOR
"BLOODY MARY"

CATHERINE DE' MEDICI
"THE BLACK QUEEN"

MARIE ANTOINETTE
"MADAME DEFICIT"

CIXI
"THE DRAGON EMPRESS"

For all of my thinking girls and boys that I've had the privilege to teach over the past twenty years. Also to my own two thinking children…Sarah and Sam. Thanks for your love, patience, and feedback. ~ **Mary Fisk Pack**

"SERPENT OF THE NILE"

Bathed in the rich orange light of the late summer sun, the Queen of Egypt reclined under a golden canopy and floated down the river on her royal barge. Beautiful servant boys fanned her, maids dressed like sea nymphs worked the ropes and rudder, while silver oars swung to the sounds of flutes, lutes, and harps. Purple sails fluttered in the wind, and wafts of the finest incense reached the shore, where crowds of people stood entranced by the spectacular sight. Cleopatra, the richest, most powerful woman in the world was definitely up to something. But what? And would her dastardly plan work? After all, they didn't call her the Serpent of the Nile for nothing.

Where she lived

Mediterranean Sea

Alexandria

Great Pyramids

Egypt

Nile River

Valley of the Kings

When she lived

This timeline shows when the Dastardly Dames were born.

69 BC	15 AD		1516 AD	1519 AD		1755 AD	1835 AD
Cleopatra	Agrippina		Mary Tudor	Catherine de' Medici		Marie Antoinette	Cixi

HER STORY

In 69 BC, a girl was born in Alexandria, Egypt, to the royal Ptolemy family. Her father, King Ptolemy XII, named her Cleopatra, which means "Glory of her Fatherland." While they were originally from Macedonia, a part of Ancient Greece, the Ptolemy family had been ruling Egypt for over 250 years.

If a capital city could be a jewel, Alexandria was the most precious of pearls. This vibrant, chaotic, and colorful city was located on the Mediterranean and had two harbors, making it a perfect trade center. Its magnificence enraptured visitors from all around the world. A wide main street, lined with rose-colored granite statues and sparkling limestone colonnades, stretched all the way to the sea. There, the Pharos lighthouse, one of the Seven Wonders of the ancient world, guided ships in and out of the Great Harbor, while goods from Africa, Asia, and beyond, arrived at its ports.

PHAROS

But Alexandria was not just an active port, it was also a renowned center for learning, attracting the greatest scholars of the time. Just as the River Nile flooded and fertilized its banks with rich silt, Alexandria flooded Cleopatra's budding intellect with a rich education. The Museon, or "Shrine of the Muses," and the Great Library of Alexandria, housing the world's largest collection of papyrus scrolls, were both within walking distance from the Ptolemy palace.

Taking her pick of tutors, Cleopatra studied literature, history, science, medicine, mathematics, and philosophy. She was incredibly articulate and mastered as many as nine languages, seamlessly switching from one to another. She was the first Ptolemy to speak Egyptian, whereas previous Ptolemies had had to rely on interpreters. In an ethnically diverse city such as Alexandria, Cleopatra was able to communicate directly with people from near and far.

This sixteenth century hand-colored engraving of the Pharos of Alexandria by Martin Heemskerck shows the legendary magnitude of the lighthouse, which rose high above the harbor and guided the way for ships miles out to sea.

This wall carving of Cleopatra at the temple of Denderah is highly stylized and doesn't tell us much about what she actually looked like.

While Cleopatra was very intelligent, she was not a stunning beauty as is commonly believed. She was described by contemporaries as having severe cheekbones, a hooked nose, and a jutting chin. The Greek historian Plutarch wrote that it was her stimulating conversation, irresistible charm, and persuasive manner that many found enchanting. She was brilliant, and that, not physical perfection, made her beautiful.

None of the statues of Cleopatra found in the world's museums has been confirmed as having been made in her lifetime. The triple uraeus—the three cobras—is thought to be her emblem, but appears on stylized statues that may not have been intended as portraits.

Portraits of Cleopatra on various coins are the only confirmed portraits of her made while she was alive.

Coins © PHGCOM/Creative Commons 3.0

When Cleopatra was eighteen, her father died. He willed his throne to Cleopatra (who became Cleopatra VII) and her ten-year-old brother, Ptolemy XIII. Cleopatra and this brother then married. This may sound strange, but marriage between brothers and sisters was common among Egyptian royalty. Even stranger, throughout their dynasty, not only did the Ptolemies marry each other, they murdered each other. "This happened by necessity in the best of families," explained the historian Plutarch.

True to her ruthless roots, Cleopatra immediately tried to take charge of the throne. Feeling understandably threatened, Cleopatra's brother/husband and his supporters drove her out of Alexandria. Cleopatra was exiled to the desert. Most princesses raised in the luxury of palace life would die under such severe conditions. Not Cleopatra. Not only did she survive, she raised a small army. She was determined to gain back the throne, and she was committed to reestablishing Egypt as a world power.

Solar disc
and horns

Vulture
headdress

Staff

Ankh, symbol
of eternal life

What she wore

The richest queen in the world, Cleopatra
would have worn extravagant jewels and
clothes. She had access to colorful Chinese
silks and fine linen; tremendous amounts
of glistening gold; and gems such as agate,
amethyst, carnelian, lapis, topaz, and pearls.

We know that Cleopatra liked to associate
herself with the goddess Isis, and often
dressed like her (shown here). It's interesting
to remember though, that Cleopatra was
actually Greek. Her everyday dress would
probably have been that of a wealthy
Greco-Roman matron of her day. Her coins
show her wearing a diadem—a broad white
ribbon tied around her forehead and knotted
at the back—the symbol of a Greek, not an
Egyptian, ruler.

Julius Caesar was never an emperor, although many people mistakenly think of him as one. He was a Roman general and politician. He became so powerful, however, that he was eventually named "Dictator for Life."

On the other side of the Mediterranean, the great generals Julius Caesar and Pompey were fighting a civil war for control of the greatest power of its day: the Roman Empire. Their war brought them to Egypt when Pompey sought refuge from Caesar. Pompey and Cleopatra's father had been friends, and Cleopatra and her brother were in power in part because of this support from Rome. Pompey probably thought he was due a return favor. But when Pompey arrived before Ptolemy, the young Egyptian king had his father's old ally beheaded on the spot. In one brutal stroke, Ptolemy had decided the fate of the Roman civil war and, or so he schemed, earned the winner's favor. Meanwhile, Cleopatra was rolling out a whole different plan.

Julius Caesar was now the ultimate broker of power in the entire Mediterranean world, and he was in Alexandria. Cleopatra needed to speak to him. The trouble was, she could not be seen anywhere near the palace where Caesar was staying as a guest, or she would be killed by her brother's men.

Rome

Mediterranean Sea

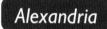

Alexandria

Nile River

Egypt

Julius Caesar's rival, Pompey, was also a Roman general and politician. He might not be as famous as Julius Caesar now, but at the time, he was every bit as formidable. In fact, some people simply referred to him as "Magnus," meaning "The Great."

Indicates Roman Empire

11

It was dusk when Cleopatra and a trusted servant rowed quietly past her brother's fleet to a private landing near the palace. There, Cleopatra had her servant roll her up in a bedroll, concealing her like a love note in a papyrus scroll. Her servant then smuggled her into the palace, and straight to Julius Caesar's room. Imagine Caesar's reaction when the Queen of Egypt was unrolled in front of him, and Cleopatra's triumph that she had pulled it off! Although he was about thirty years older than she was, and married, Julius Caesar was a fit fighter (albeit a bit sensitive about his balding head) and known to be a flirt.

Cleopatra has been variously said to have been hidden in a bedroll, a laundry sack, or—Hollywood's preferred version and the one illustrated here—a carpet.

No one knows exactly what the two talked about that night. Some said that it was love at first sight. They certainly had a lot in common, both being highly educated and powerful rulers. Egypt had wealth. Rome had military strength. Together they could rule the world! But others believed that Cleopatra only bewitched Julius Caesar for her own ends. One thing is certain, Caesar first put pressure on Ptolemy XIII to rule with Cleopatra, and then when the boy king would hear nothing of it, he waged war, defeated the king (who disappeared; his body was never found), took captive her scheming younger sister, Arsinoe (who had been declared Queen), and reinstalled Cleopatra on the throne.

This limestone plaque was dedicated to Cleopatra and depicts her making an offering to the goddess Isis. That's Cleopatra on the right, shown as a traditional male pharaoh. You may also be surprised to notice that the inscription is in Greek. We tend to forget that the Ptolemies were Greek.

To flaunt that she was back in charge and to impress Julius Caesar with Egypt's abundance, Cleopatra and Caesar cruised the fertile Nile against a colorful backdrop—the lush green grass of the riverbanks, golden grain fields, trees heavy with ripening fruit, spectacular purple sunsets.

Complementing her country's fruitfulness, Cleopatra gave birth to a son named Caesarion later that year. To commemorate the birth—and the union of Egyptian wealth with Roman power—Cleopatra minted special coins that portrayed her as Isis, the cherished goddess of love and protector of children.

What she ate

As royalty, Cleopatra was sure to eat the finest foods grown in Egypt and traded from other lands. Foods at her elaborate feasts included roasted wild boar, fish, duck, goose, peacock, oysters, sea urchins, olives, nuts—like walnuts and chestnuts—a variety of vegetables such as peas, beans, on-ions, garlic, leeks, lettuce, cabbages, turnips, and crisp lotus roots. Lentils were a staple as were grains, such as wheat and barley. The best of these were stored at the Royal Granaries.

This head, thought to be of Caesarion, was discovered by Franck Goddio, a famous underwater archaeologist, at the bottom of the sea off Alexandria.

Just how wealthy was she?

People have tried to calculate how rich Cleopatra would have been in modern terms. It is almost impossible to arrive at an accurate number, but in her own day, stories were circulating about how she could afford to dissolve her pearls in vinegar in order to win a bet or make a point, and how she bathed only in asses' milk. It's fairly safe to say she was one of the richest people of her time, and quite possibly of all time.

Julius Caesar was just as pleased with his new son. When he returned to Rome, he summoned Cleopatra and baby Caesarion to follow him and installed them in their own villa, ignoring the grumbles of a scandalized Rome. (Caesar was married, after all. So was Cleopatra; she'd married her other brother, and he even accompanied her to Rome). A fleet of ships carried everything from Cleopatra's extensive retinue, to gifts of gold, cinnamon, jars of Nile water (known to be an elixir), leopards, and even a giraffe. Cleopatra, after all, had an image to uphold.

Caesar's mistress, the Queen of Egypt, caused quite a stir in a city that was rustic compared to elegant Alexandria. She was foreign. She was smart and independent. She was royal, even divine. She was richer than any Roman. It was rumored she wore on her earlobes the two largest pearls in the world, and that it would not be beyond her to dissolve them in vinegar and swallow them, such was her reckless extravagance. And when Cleopatra's sister Arsinoe, to some the rightful Queen of Egypt, was paraded through the streets in golden shackles along with Caesar's other war spoils, the Romans thought she was not just reckless but heartless, too.

So when Julius Caesar erected a golden statue of Cleopatra next to a public statue of Venus, the Roman goddess of love, his countrymen were incensed. Surely this extravagant Egyptian queen was inspiring Caesar's growing arrogance. What the Romans could not abide was Caesar playing the god king, wearing triumphal dress and seating himself on a raised golden chair that looked an awful lot like a throne, something unheard of in Roman government. Some of Caesar's fellow senators were so outraged by what they saw as Caesar's intention to make himself king, they stabbed him to death in the senate chamber.

"Death of Julius Caesar," painted by Vincenzo Camuccini in 1798, shows an imagined scene of Caesar's assassination. Julius Caesar was stabbed twenty-three times.

With her protector, lover, and the father of her only child murdered, Cleopatra fled back to Alexandria as soon as her fleet could sail, fearing for her own life and that of her son. Back at home, she had her brother/husband poisoned, and she proclaimed three-year-old Caesarion her new co-regent. The new King of Egypt was Roman, a brilliant strategy to strengthen the bond between Egypt and Rome at a tenuous time.

Few would have guessed on Julius Caesar's death that his nineteen-year-old heir would grow up to be Rome's first—and some would say greatest—emperor, often simply referred to as Augustus (The Revered).

The ancient historian, Plutarch, thought of Mark Antony as a man of great strengths—loyal, generous, and brave—and equally great weaknesses—reckless and irresponsible.

Rome was once again plunged into civil war, with two camps eventually forming behind Octavian, Julius Caesar's teenaged great-nephew—whom he'd officially adopted—and heir, and the dashing Mark Antony, Julius Caesar's friend and second in command (who once rode through Rome on a chariot pulled by lions). Once again, Cleopatra had to choose which of two Roman men could best guarantee her own, and Egypt's, independence.

After a bloody battle, Mark Antony was victorious, while an ailing Octavian returned to Rome. It looked as though Mark Antony, the handsome curly-haired general with the Herculean physique, would be Cleopatra's choice. She needed his protection. He needed her money. He summoned her to meet him again and again. But she would respond only when she was ready.

To impress Mark Antony, Cleopatra conjured up something spectacular. After traveling 700 miles across the Mediterranean to where he was stationed, she dressed as the goddess Venus and sailed the last few miles toward him in a royal barge trimmed in gold and rowed with silver oars. The sails bloomed purple—the imperial color of Rome—while under a golden canopy, Cleopatra lay back, fanned by young boys dressed to look like cupids. Her plan worked beautifully. Mark Antony joined Cleopatra, knee-deep in roses, for a lavish feast beneath an intricate canopy of lights. Soon, she appeared to have him wrapped around her finger. One of his first love-struck acts: eliminating the other Egyptian queen. Mark Antony had Arsinoe removed from the Temple of Artemis in the city of Ephesus, where she'd sought asylum, and murdered on its marble steps.

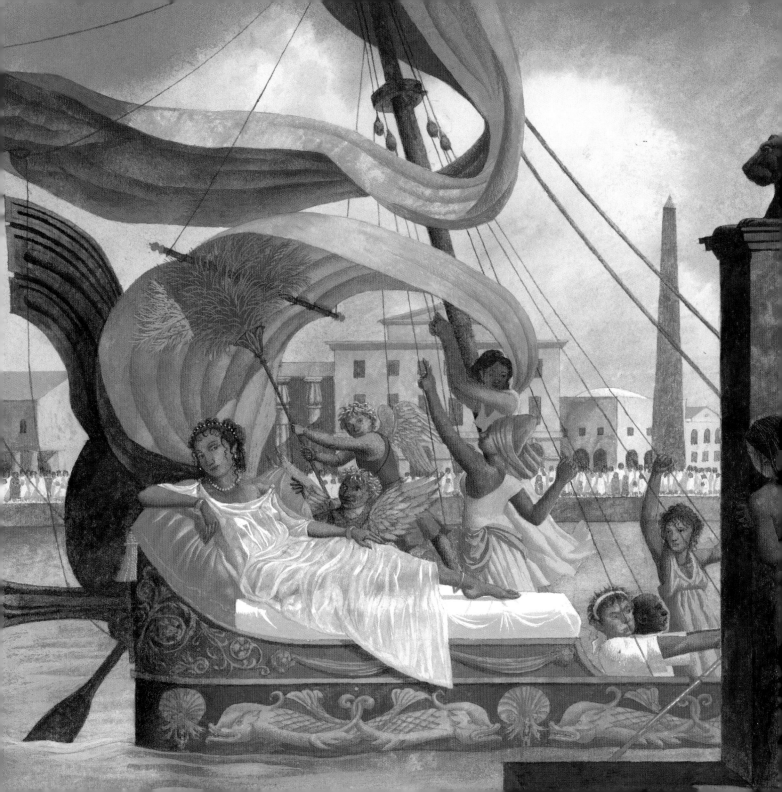

But politics was politics, and Octavian, whose power had only grown while Mark Antony was cavorting with Cleopatra, was looking difficult to beat. So, Mark Antony went back to Rome to marry Octavian's beloved and beautiful sister, Octavia. Marriage to Octavia signaled an alliance between the two men, an agreement to share power.

Left behind in Egypt, Cleopatra gave birth to twins—a boy named Alexander, after Alexander the Great, and a girl she named Cleopatra Selene. With the birth of her children came brighter days. The Nile flooded and Egypt's crops were once again abundant, which strengthened Cleopatra's goddess image and won her the adoration of her people.

© Giovanni Dall'Orto/WikiCommons

All in the family: Coins featuring Mark Antony and Octavian, and Mark Antony and Octavia, whose portrait bust is shown above.

In fact, over three years would go by before Mark Antony and Cleopatra saw each other again. A war against the Parthians brought Mark Antony back to the East, and he sent for Cleopatra. Confident he'd triumph in this latest conquest and happy to see his family—including the twins he was meeting for the first time—Mark Antony granted Cleopatra and their children land that belonged to Rome, extending her territories to include parts of modern-day Lebanon, Libya, and Turkey, and the island of Crete. Cleopatra now ruled over nearly the entire eastern Mediterranean coast. She had come a long way from being exiled in the desert and disguised in a bedroll. She had regained her throne and expanded Egypt's land, and thus Egyptian power. From now on, Cleopatra and Mark Antony were inseparable.

Cleopatra declared a new era in Egypt, renaming herself, "Queen Cleopatra, the Goddess, the Younger, Father-Loving and Fatherland-Loving." Surrounded by their children, including a new son, she and Mark Antony presided on golden thrones over a citywide celebration of their mighty empire—she as the New Isis, wearing a crown of cobras, he as Dionysus. According to one historian, they were "the two most magnificent people in the world." But not to the Romans, who believed Mark Antony's growing arrogance and grandiosity was reminiscent of another, former, ruler who had been seduced by the very same queen.

The lands that Mark Antony granted Cleopatra and their children.

The two sides of this coin show Mark Antony not with Octavia, but with Cleopatra.

This painting by Lorenzo A. Castro, painted in 1672, contrasts the beauty of the morning light at sea with the ferocity of the great Battle of Actium.

While Mark Antony played god in Alexandria, back in Rome, Octavian seized the opportunity to get rid of this unwanted partner he'd been shackled with. He denounced Mark Antony as a traitor and painted Cleopatra as an evil, scheming seductress. Warning that Cleopatra would conquer Rome as she had conquered Mark Antony, Octavian declared war, but only on Cleopatra—a savvy political move. This way he wasn't declaring war on a fellow Roman who still commanded a loyal following. And he knew that said fellow Roman was so infatuated, he would side with his lover and fight against his homeland. A brilliant plan.

On September 2nd, 31 BC, the two sides clashed at Actium in a naval battle that raged throughout the morning with no clear winner. When the afternoon winds whipped up, Cleopatra retreated, leading her fleet back toward Alexandria, where, despite her obvious losses, she had her ships garlanded in flowers as if returning in triumph. Even more shockingly, Mark Antony followed her, abandoning his men in the middle of the battle; they had no other choice but to surrender.

Cleopatra and Mark Antony must have known that their eventual defeat was certain. Cleopatra, who could not bear to see her throne taken away yet, went on a spree, killing her detractors and confiscating great sums of money, gold, jewels, and treasures, which she stored in her newly built mausoleum. While an inconsolable Mark Antony exiled himself to a small hut at the base of the great lighthouse, Cleopatra plotted their escape. She gathered a motley army of allies—neighboring tribesmen, thieves, friendly kings—much as she'd done as a girl in the desert. She had her ships lifted out of the Mediterranean and hauled across land to the Red Sea, in an effort to flee to India or Spain, where she and Mark Antony could make a new life. But it was of no use; her ships were set afire, and she returned to Alexandria, just as Octavian was making landfall in her beloved city.

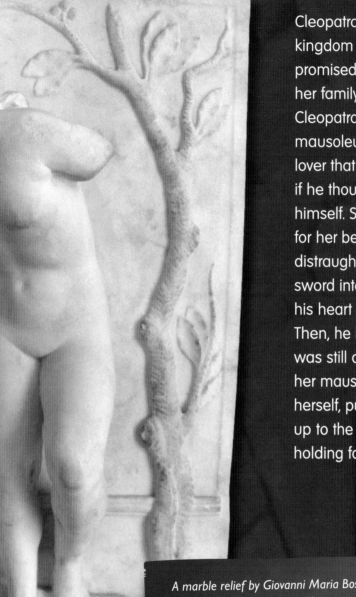

Cleopatra's sole goal now was to save the kingdom and the lives of her children. Octavian promised Cleopatra he would pardon her and her family if she had Mark Antony murdered. Cleopatra rushed to her treasure-filled mausoleum and sent a message to her lover that she was dead. She believed that if he thought she was dead, he would kill himself. She would sacrifice her beloved for her beloved Egypt. As expected, a distraught Mark Antony plunged his sword into his chest, only, he missed his heart and did not die immediately. Then, he learned that Cleopatra was still alive. He was brought to her mausoleum where Cleopatra, herself, pulled his wounded body up to the platform where she was holding fort. He died in her arms.

A marble relief by Giovanni Maria Bosca, carved around 1520-1530, shows various elements of the lovers' tragic end, which is often wrongly remembered as a double suicide. In reality, their deaths were separated by a week or two.

Afraid that Cleopatra would kill herself and destroy all of her treasures—treasures he desperately needed to fund his newly won empire—Octavian had Cleopatra captured alive and her treasures carted away. But then it is believed that Cleopatra escaped and snuck back to her mausoleum where she finally, dramatically, took her own life. The story (and one Shakespeare play) has it that a basket of sweet Egyptian figs was brought to her with a poisonous asp (an Egyptian cobra) hidden in it. Cleopatra laid the asp on her bared breast and died from its venomous bite.

Although such an ending would certainly befit the Serpent of the Nile, it is highly improbable. Cleopatra more likely took a quicker and surer route: poison. Either way, at the age of thirty-nine, the last Queen of Egypt was dead, and with her died Egyptian independence. Egypt, the magnificent land of the pharaohs, became just another Roman province.